Seven Last Words
for
Seven Weeks

Seven Last Words *for* Seven Weeks

PRAYING WITH JESUS ON THE CROSS

Mary Sweeney, SC

Illustrated by Julie Lonneman

Paulist Press
New York/Mahwah, NJ

Cover design by Sharyn Banks
Book design by Lynn Else

Library of Congress Cataloging-in-Publication Data

Sweeney, Mary, 1948-
    Seven last words for seven weeks : praying with Jesus on the cross / Mary Sweeney ; illustrated by Julie Lonneman.
      p. cm.
    Includes bibliographical references.
    ISBN 0-8091-4436-0 (alk. paper)
    1. Lent. 2. Lent—Prayer-books and devotions—English. 3. Catholic Church—Prayer-books and devotions—English. 4. Spiritual retreats. I. Title.
    BX2170.L4S94 2007
    242'.34—dc22

2006021818

Published by Paulist Press
997 Macarthur Boulevard
Mahwah, New Jersey 07430

www.paulistpress.com

Printed and bound in the United States of America

Contents

In memory of my parents

Edward and Catherine (Glasheen) Sweeney

who first taught Theresa, Ed, and me
the spirit and practices of Lent

Acknowledgments

Although this is a small book, it seems to have taken twenty years to come into being and so it carries with it a debt of gratitude. Over those years, I was blessed by the support of many people, in particular the members of my religious congregation, the Sisters of Charity of Halifax, who continue to "show forth the love of God." I'm grateful to them and to the members of the faith communities at both Boston University, where I ministered from 1986 to 1995, and at the Newman Center/Our Lady of Wisdom Parish at the University of Maine in Orono, where I ministered from 1996 to 2003. Their invitations to preach in the service of the Seven Last Words and the suggestion that I publish those reflections have brought forth this book.

For their encouragement and suggestions, my thanks go to Barbara Bader Aldave; James W. Donovan, CSP; Ann Marie (Hayes) Boltz; Charles J. Healey, SJ; Katarina Schuth, OSF; and Terri Wlodarski. For answering my questions with ease and humor, I'm grateful to Kevin Carrizo di Camillo of Paulist Press; for sharing her creative vision, I thank Julie Lonneman whose illustrations enhance these pages. A word of thanks goes to the members of the Boston College community where I currently serve as campus minister, to the librarians there, and especially to Joseph M. O'Keefe, SJ, whose invitation to preach at St. Ignatius Church in 1986 planted the seeds for these reflections.

INTRODUCTION

Early in the Lenten season of 1986 when I was a student at Weston Jesuit School of Theology, a friend, Jesuit classmate Joe O'Keefe, now dean of the Lynch School of Education at Boston College, invited me to participate in the service of the Seven Last Words at Saint Ignatius Parish in Chestnut Hill, Mass., where he was serving as transitional deacon that year. Eager for an opportunity to share a reflection on scripture, a rare opportunity then for a woman in ministry in the Catholic Church, I accepted the invitation. Joe promptly assigned me my "word": "I am thirsty" (John 19:28).

The service of the Seven Last Words consists of music, silence, prayer, and reflections offered on each of the seven last words (which are not really words but sentences) that Jesus spoke from the cross. No single gospel account contains all seven sentences; rather, they are compiled from the four gospels, and they capture the experiences of the dying Jesus. Typically, the service lasts from noon until 3:00 p.m. on Good Friday, and members of the congregation come and go as their schedules allow.

When Joe assigned me the verse, he gave me a kind of gift that I couldn't have anticipated: I had six weeks to pray with that one phrase, to sit with it, to run it through my mind, to allow the news of the day to filter through it. It was such a brief phrase, so highly portable, so easy to remember, that praying with it became a simple part of my everyday activities. There was no text to track down, no book to carry: The gift was the simplicity of my prayer for that Lenten season.[1] For several years after that, I was involved in the service of the Seven Last Words at various churches and campuses. Each time I had the word early in the season, I found a certain ease in praying with it for the weeks that led up to Good Friday.

In 2002, while I was serving as a campus minister for the community at Our Lady of Wisdom Parish/the Newman Center for the University of Maine in Orono, I wanted to create a program that would help the members of that community establish some kind of regular time for daily prayer in their busy schedules. I remembered my experience with John 19:28. Now, however, I wanted a program that would facilitate sharing among the participants, many of whom would be making a commitment to daily meditative prayer for the first time. I also wanted it to be a format in which they could encourage one another to persevere in that commitment. This book is based on that program and format. The format is meant to enable participants to carry one *word* with them for a week, then have an opportunity to talk about how it helped them in prayer. The program is intended to last the seven weeks of Lent, inviting participants to pray one *word* each week.

Again and again the members of the groups talked about how difficult it was to set aside ten or fifteen minutes. In discovering their common challenges, the participants took heart. One day, I asked quite simply, "If I called you, would you talk to me for fifteen minutes?" The unsuspecting woman quickly responded, "Of course!" Then she realized my point.

Phone calls are a helpful image for another reason. They often come unexpectedly and they free us to express things spontaneously. So, too, with this way of praying with a word: While planned times for prayer are important, the "portability" of a word enables participants to lift their hearts and their minds to God in a very spontaneous way wherever they are, whenever the Spirit moves them. Between such spontaneous prayer and planned prayer, there is a mutual reinforcement of the heart's desire and a strengthening of one's relationship with God.

In addition to the shared insights and prayers from the scriptural texts, the very practical points that came up in the groups were helpful: "Where did you pray?" "Did you use a candle or listen to music to help you to be still?" "Where did you put the paper/booklet for the program to remind you to pray?" Of course there was a lot of laughter, too, when people shared their successes and their failures. Week by week, as participants shared their insights and their very practical points, there was a sense of being involved in a *common* pursuit, one that was beneficial but also challenging. To see their neighbors, colleagues, and fellow parishioners struggle to create a time for prayer in their lives was a great gift.

Part of the book is repetitious by design. Many of us are all too aware of the difficulty of keeping to a schedule or routine for prayer, of setting aside a set amount of time daily to tend our relationship with God. The repetition of "Don't get discouraged," may be as useful for the veteran as it is for the novice.

The program fits well into the Lenten season. Although there are six full weeks in the season and seven words for reflection, most parishes begin to prepare the community for

Seven Last Words for Seven Weeks

Lent in advance. The ideal is to begin the program the week of Ash Wednesday. The first word gives the participants an occasion to consider their own spiritual thirst and to recognize that this is an opportunity to do something to satisfy that thirst during Lent.

Since my first experience in preaching in the Seven Last Words service, I have participated in many similar services on Good Friday, often in ecumenical settings at Boston University and the University of Maine. Parts of the reflections I share in this book are drawn from those homilies. Some selections are drawn from other sources.

Although I created this program with small group dynamics in mind, I hope that it will be beneficial to those who are following it by themselves.

I believe that during the seasons of Advent and Lent, the Spirit blesses the church with a communal desire to deepen our relationship with God. There is an energy that draws us to renewed devotion. As you begin this season of Lent, may you know the Spirit's blessing. May all who use these reflections know deeper faith, richer hope, and stronger love that will lead to the joy of the resurrection.

Mary Sweeney, SC

"I AM THIRSTY."

The Week of
Ash Wednesday:
THE FIRST WORD

After this, when Jesus knew that all was now
finished, he said (in order to fulfill the scripture),
"I am thirsty." (John 19:28)

What a common human experience these words of
Jesus convey. "I am thirsty." It is an experience we all know
well from childhood to advanced age. We know the call of
children from their beds: "Can I have a glass of water?" We
know, too, the elderly hospital patient too weak to moisten
her own lips. And we know our own healthy thirsts after vig-
orous exercising or after a salty meal.

Sometimes our thirst is merely a slight distraction until
we find a water fountain; other times our thirst may become
an obsession: We have to find water, and we drink more and
more until we have finally slaked our thirst. So we know something of the thirst that Jesus experiences in this verse from
John's Gospel. It is the thirst of a man who cannot satisfy his
own need. He is dependent on those who hear his cry. But

from another chapter of John's Gospel, there is something else that causes us to reflect: This is the same Jesus who, at the well with the Samaritan woman, offered her living water, water to quench her thirst forever (John 4:10), and who cried "Let anyone who is thirsty come to me" (John 7:37).

A cruel irony we have before us: A vibrant man who once offered living water is now reduced to a dying man who cannot relieve his own thirst. Within him, signs of refreshment and vitality are contrasted with dryness and death. He who in John's Gospel spoke of himself as living bread, light of life, and source of living water now hangs on a cross, incapable of satisfying even his *own* needs. How could he ever be the source of life and light and refreshment for anyone *else*?

This Jesus, teacher, prophet, miracle worker, knows well the limitations of human life. He who "emptied himself, taking the form of a slave" (Phil 2:7), acutely experiences the poverty of human living in the experience of human dying. Mocked, scourged, and spat upon, he knows the helplessness of our living and our dying. He has accepted the limitation of being truly human. In this acceptance he has embraced us in our humanity, and in this embrace that takes us in with our blessing and our sin, he is embraced by the Father. Jesus becomes the exalted one, source of life, light, and refreshment.

I recall sitting with a group of people who were participating in a program aimed at integrating prayer and social justice. We tried to answer the question, "For what do you thirst?" Responses in the group varied. One young woman thirsted for freedom. Bogged down by study and work, she longed to be free to enjoy the good things of her life. Another participant thirsted for intimacy: a human longing to share deeply with another. A third longed to savor beauty in life, perhaps to counter the ugliness and the dirt that seem to surround us at times and to penetrate our own lives. For what do *you* thirst? What or who will satisfy *your* heart's desire?

The psalms, the song-prayers of Judaism, capture the longing for God in an image of thirst. "As a deer longs for flowing streams, so my soul longs for you, O God; my soul thirsts for God" (Ps 42:1, 2). Such longing for God may lie deep within our hearts. We may recognize that longing frequently, or we may not recognize it, or we may translate it into something else. Sometimes our other thirsts get in the way. And sometimes, when other things have failed to satisfy us, we begin to understand something more profound about our lives.

For what do you thirst? Can you be attentive to the words of Jesus as they reveal your own thirst?

Each day this week:

+ Try to set aside fifteen minutes. Find or create quiet space where you can pray. Spend some time just paying attention to your breathing and growing still. Then ask for the Holy Spirit to help you to pray.

+ Recall the words of Jesus: "I am thirsty." Try to be attentive to that scene in the gospel. You may want to be a compassionate observer or you may want to speak to Jesus.

+ At the conclusion of your prayer time, express your gratitude for the time that you've had. If you find it helpful, jot down a word or a few words about your prayer/reflection.

+ Carry the gospel word with you during the week. Call it to mind when you're walking or running; showering or doing the dishes; ironing or standing in line; drinking a glass of water or feeling thirsty.

+ The most important advice: *Don't get discouraged.* Simply do the best you can. Some days you may be able to set aside fifteen minutes and feel blessed. Be thankful. Other days, it may be a struggle just to remember what the word is. Be thankful that you desire to pray. Don't give up. Do what you can. Speak to God about your joy or your frustration in prayer. Ask for God's help to set aside the time you need.

Here are some thoughts and questions for your consideration during the week. Use them if they're helpful. Disregard them if they aren't.

+ Recall your own experiences of thirst. How do they help you to relate to this scene of Jesus on the cross? In your prayer, express to him how you feel.

The Week of Ash Wednesday

✦ Consider the people around the world who suffer because of the poor quality of water or the inadequate supply of water. Remember them to Jesus in prayer. Remember/imagine the face of Jesus.

✦ How does the suffering of Jesus move you? Share your feelings with him.

✦ For what do you thirst this Lenten season? Can you name it? Can you ask for it?

✦ How is Jesus living water for you?

"FATHER, FORGIVE THEM; FOR THEY DO NOT KNOW WHAT THEY ARE DOING."

The First Week of Lent:
THE SECOND WORD

Then Jesus said, *"Father, forgive them;*
for they do not know what they are doing."
(Luke 23:34)

In the early 1990s, I was privileged to hear the late Father Lawrence Martin Jenco speak. His is a powerful story of forgiveness, and it is told in his book *Bound to Forgive*.[2] Father Jenco had been named program director for Catholic Relief Services in Lebanon in 1984. In January 1985, he was kidnapped and, along with several other men, held hostage in Lebanon for more than a year and a half by Iranian terrorists. Several years later, Father Jenco spoke about what happened when, shortly before his release, he came face to face with one of his captors. The captor, Sayeed, asked Father Jenco if he could forgive him for what he had done to him. Father Jenco said that he could; but then he asked Sayeed to forgive him. Father Jenco told his captor, "Sayeed, there were times I hated you. I was filled with anger and revenge for what you did to me and my brothers. But Jesus said on the mountain top that I was not to hate you. I was to love you. Sayeed, I need to ask God's forgiveness and yours."

I don't think I'm alone when I say that Christ's command to forgive those who have sinned against us is one of the most challenging dimensions of Christianity. When we have been hurt it's so easy to want to reply in kind, to revert to the old teaching of an "eye for eye, a tooth for tooth" (Exod 21:24). It's so much more difficult to try to forgive, or to turn the other cheek and even to allow the other person to hurt us again. Yet that is the teaching of Jesus Christ. How often are we to forgive? "[S]eventy-seven times" (Matt 18:22), Jesus tells us in what may be a bit of hyperbole. Still, we get the point. But we all know, from our own hearts, oftentimes from our own family relationships, how holding on to hurt, nourishing more bitterness, carrying long-standing grudges are what happen.

We know, too, that such attitudes take more of a toll on us than the initial hurt. Our hands, our personalities, and our hearts become misshapen: At times we see our hands shaped into fists; we see our personalities become cynical and spiteful; we see our hearts shrivel and close to love. How often it seems that the initial hurt is far less significant than the subsequent wall that is built upon it. Grudges intensify, and family members or friends, neighbors or colleagues go their separate ways, forgetting why their relationship ruptured, remembering only to honor the rupture, instead of turning to reconciliation.

The words of Jesus encourage us to look again into our own hearts to understand how we feel toward others who have hurt us. A dying man faces his tormentors and forgives them. And not only does he forgive them; he intercedes on their behalf with God. This example of Jesus asks us to see the other as one like us: in need of prayer and forgiveness.

Can you recall a hurt that has taken hold of you, one that you can't seem to let go? Have you noticed how it can drain your energy and attention? How it can make you into the sort of person that you really don't want to be?

As you meditate on the words of Jesus this week, consider how he invites you to follow his example.

Each day this week:

+ Try to set aside fifteen minutes. Settling down may be your greatest challenge. Focus on your breathing or try to sing a simple, slow refrain from a hymn. Notice how your breathing slows down. Ask the Holy Spirit to help you to hear this word and to understand how it touches your life this week.

+ Recall the words of Jesus: "Father, forgive them; for they know not what they are doing." Try to imagine that scene in the gospel.

+ At the conclusion of your prayer time, express your thanks that you have been able to be attentive—to whatever degree—to the words and message of Jesus. Again, if it's helpful, you may want to jot down what this word means to you at this point in your life.

Seven Last Words for Seven Weeks

✦ During the week, you may find that new insights about forgiveness come to you as you go about your daily life. You may think of this word when you see someone who has offended you or when you feel hurt or frustrated.

✦ The most important advice: Don't get discouraged. Do the best you can. Try to honor what you've already learned about when and where it's helpful for you to pray. If you feel frustrated, speak to God about that frustration. Ask for help to make time for prayer, if that's a struggle for you.

✦ Teresa of Avila defined prayer as a heart-to-heart conversation with the One by whom we know ourselves to be loved. Is that a comforting definition for you?

Here are some thoughts and questions for your consideration. If they're helpful, use them; if they're not helpful, disregard them.

✦ Imagine this gospel scene. Speak to Jesus about his forgiveness for those who have hurt him.

✦ How does this prayer of Jesus influence the way in which Jesus dies?

✦ Most days we find something impersonal or someone anonymous who offends or disturbs or annoys us: the person playing loud music, the driver who cuts us off or who fails to signal a turn, the inconsiderate stranger who does something that grates on us. Can we find in Jesus a way to forgive and to move on joyfully with our lives?

✦ Within our closest relationships, with family members, friends, colleagues, community members, we often find the source of our deepest hurts. Infidelity, slander, disregard, abandonment, insensitivity—all may trigger our anger and our desire for revenge. In the suffering Jesus, we find another approach. Who has offended you? For whom, with the help of God, do you want to pray?

✦ Recall the thirst, the desire that prompted you to commit yourself to prayer during Lent. Continue to express that desire to God.

"WOMAN, HERE IS YOUR SON."
"HERE IS YOUR MOTHER."

The Second Week of Lent:
THE THIRD WORD

When Jesus saw his mother and the disciple
whom he loved standing beside her, he said to his
mother, *"Woman, here is your son."* Then he said
to the disciple, *"Here is your mother."* And from
that hour the disciple took her into his own home.
(John 19:26, 27)

Of all the phrases we hear in the service of the Seven
Last Words of Jesus, I think that there are none so tender as
the words of Jesus spoken to his mother and to his beloved
disciple. These words of a dying man touch so familiarly on
human life—in birth, in friendship, and in death—and
demonstrate such common human emotion that it seems
quite possible that any one of us could utter them or something similar in our last moments. They reveal the God-Man
deeply embedded in his human experience—caught in the
connectedness, the caring, and the community that each one
of us, if we are fortunate, knows from our earliest days.

Seven Last Words for Seven Weeks

The Jesus of John's Gospel has strong human ties. Throughout the first part of the gospel, we see evidence of his connectedness: He invites people to join him, to walk along with him, to spend time with him. He attends a wedding; he is part of a group of close friends at Bethany. He cries at the death of his friend Lazarus. In the latter part of the gospel, he stresses his desire for union with his followers when he prays. He speaks of their abiding in him, and he in them. This Jesus is not an isolated individual. He is part of a fabric of many threads; he is deeply and variously tied to others, and that connectedness exacts a price. It is the price of caring about and caring for those he loves. Now he is about to die. How shall he provide for his mother? He entrusts her to his disciple John, the one whom he loved.

This gesture is so important to Jesus that it seems as if it had loomed as the last piece of unfinished business of his earthly life. In John's Gospel, after Jesus has made provision for Mary following his death, the next verse tells us, he "knew that all was now finished" (John 19:28.) He has done all that he had to do. There is, perhaps, a kind of relief in that handing over, in that act of entrusting. It seems to provide a peacefulness that community, at its best, is meant to ensure: At the crucial moment in our woundedness, we all want to have someone whom we trust to whom we can say, "Please help me… please take care of this for me." In that sharing of our burden, we are mindful of our weakness and of the blessing of those who stand by us.

Does the pain of this mother touch our hearts? What in our world helps us to understand Mary's anguish, Mary's motherly love? Back in 1993, in one more of the many tragic chapters in the story of modern Ireland, a bomb planted by members of the Irish Republican Party exploded in a British shopping mall. Among its victims were two boys, Tim Parry, age twelve, and Jonathan Ball, age three. It was a mother in the Republic of Ireland who expressed what so many have felt. Susan McHugh of Dublin, herself the mother of three children, felt an outrage as she saw two young, innocent lives taken. She felt empathy, too, as she imagined the grief of the boys' mothers. She was instrumental in creating a demonstration for peace—an effort to end the terrorism of the IRA. It was an enormous demonstration, drawing twenty-thousand participants. When Susan McHugh was questioned about her activism, she responded in a language that in itself is disarming: "I'm an ordinary mum, a housewife."[3] And that was enough for her to say.

We see mothers mourning on the news almost every night: mothers in the Middle East, in Africa, in the subcontinent, in inner cities, in the suburbs. Can we look at them and empathize? Can we look at them and be drawn into some action? Can they entrust to us, the members of the world community, their story and their pleas for justice and food and for an end to all the senseless killing?

Perhaps the very tenderness of this gospel scene of a dying son, a grieving mother, and a trusted friend will move us, helping us to see how Christ's love makes family and friend of us all.

Each day this week:

✦ Try to set aside fifteen minutes. Again, notice your breathing. Take note, too, of any tension in your body and try to relax. Ask for the Holy Spirit to help you to pray. Ask Mary to intercede for you as you pray. Is there a favorite hymn that might help? A mantra that would help you to focus?

✦ Recall the gospel scene of John 19:26, 27. Try to be attentive to details of that scene.

✦ At the conclusion of your prayer time, express your thanks to God. If you think it would be helpful, spend some time at the end of this week recording in a journal your thoughts and prayers and the things that have helped you to be attentive.

✦ There will be many times when you see parents and children together this week; some will be in happy circumstances, some in challenging, maybe even tragic, circumstances. Such sights may be a reminder of this gospel scene and may help you to lift your heart and your mind to God.

✦ If you're not able to make the time that you want to pray, don't get discouraged. Do the best you can.

✦ The *Baltimore Catechism* taught many generations of Catholics a very simple definition of prayer. "Prayer is the lifting up of our minds and hearts to God."[4] Does that definition match your experience of prayer?

The Second Week of Lent

+ Edward Farrell wrote a book entitled *Prayer Is a Hunger*.[5] Have you ever thought of prayer in that way?

During the week, some additional questions may be helpful for your reflection that leads to conversation with Jesus, Mary, or John, the beloved disciple.

+ How might this scene help you to care for the people whom you love in your life?

+ Do you feel free to ask others for help? Are there certain circumstances or certain people that make it easier or more difficult to ask?

+ How does this gospel scene impress you as an adult child? How does it touch you as a parent? Watch the news, read the paper, and recognize the faces of other parents who suffer because of their children's suffering. Pray for them.

+ How do you relate to Mary, the mother of Jesus? What example of encouragement does her life offer you? Pray the Hail Mary thoughtfully:

Hail Mary, full of grace. The Lord is with you.
Blessed are you among women
And blessed is the fruit of your womb, Jesus.
Holy Mary, mother of God,
Pray for us sinners
Now and at the hour of our death. Amen.

"ELI, ELI, LEMA SABACHTHANI?" "MY GOD, MY GOD, WHY HAVE YOU FORSAKEN ME?"

The Third Week of Lent:
THE FOURTH WORD

And about three o'clock
Jesus cried with a loud voice,
"Eli, Eli, lema sabachthani?" that is,
"My God, my God, why have you forsaken me?"
(Matt 27:46)

Sometimes, for Christians, the cross seems to lose its value, its drama, its tragedy. It adorns our churches and our walls or finds a home in our jewelry boxes. But during this season we try to get back in touch with what the cross really means.

"My God, my God, why have you forsaken me?" are words that help us to grasp the meaning of the cross. These words of emotional pain capture the reality of the suffering and death of Jesus. But they do more than that. They remind us of how he identified with our sufferings. In our dark moments, we, too, may feel abandoned by God. We, too, may feel that we are alone in our pain. Can we, in those moments, remember these words?

If you consult your Bible, you'll find that these words that Jesus utters in the Gospels of Matthew and Mark are the opening words of Psalm 22. Jesus is praying the psalm of a suffering person who, although feeling abandoned by God, continues to cry to God: "Why are you so far from helping me...? I am a worm, and not human" (Ps 22:1b, 6). The psalmist stays in the conversation. Isn't that what we all need to do? Yes, we may feel abandoned by God at times, but we also know, deep in our hearts, that it's better to rail against God than to turn and walk away; it's better to stay in the conversation than to harden our hearts.

The wonderful thing about Psalm 22 is that we sense the person's strong relationship with God in the face of intense suffering. A turning point comes and the psalmist longs to proclaim God's name in the midst of the people, for God has neither spurned nor disdained the sufferer, but rather God is attentive.

Seeing the suffering Jesus and hearing how he prayed helps us to pray our way through our own sufferings. We realize again that he really entered into our human living and took on our heartaches and our pain.

The Third Week of Lent

In her brief poem, Miriam Kessler puts it succinctly:

My God, My God, he cried,
if he is quoted right....
Somehow that moan is comforting
to us, alone at night,
who tremble, daring dawn,
that He, so wise and strong,
should weep and ask for aid.
   Somehow, my lovely distant god,
   it makes me less afraid.

"Eli, Eli" by Miriam Kessler
in *Cries of the Spirit* [6]

Each day this week:

+ Try to set aside fifteen minutes. What helps you to be
  still? Take a few minutes to gather, or to "recollect,"
  yourself.

+ Ask for the Spirit to help you to pray.

+ Recall the scene in the gospel above. Think of Jesus
  as he uttered the words, "My God, my God, why have
  you forsaken me?" How does *your* heart respond to
  him?

+ At the conclusion of your prayer time, thank God for
  the desire to pray and, if it's helpful, jot down what
  was in your heart.

✦ As you go through this week, carry the word with you. Call it to mind when you're going about your usual activities, while you're waiting for someone. Call it to mind when you're feeling alone or abandoned or when you're thinking about others who may feel abandoned.

✦ Don't get discouraged if you're having trouble making the time for quiet prayer. Do the best you can. Carry the word with you, and you may be surprised at how frequently you find yourself praying spontaneously.

✦ Pray for others who are in the group, and pray that together you may encourage one another.

✦ When he was a Paulist priest, James Carroll, the American novelist and columnist, wrote several books about prayer. In *Prayer from Where We Are*,[7] he described prayer as being attentive to the presence of God, being tender with the presence of God, tending the presence of God. Do these different ways of describing prayer help you?

Once again, here are some thoughts and questions for your consideration. Use them if they are helpful. Disregard them if they aren't.

34

The Third Week of Lent

+ As you imagine this gospel scene, can you enter into conversation with Jesus about his suffering?

+ Do you have your own experiences of feeling abandoned by God? How did/does it feel? How did/do you relate to God in those situations?

+ Pray for those who feel abandoned: spouses and children who have been deserted, the mentally ill and homeless who are uncared for, those who cling to ideals when others have folded to pressure.

+ Pray in gratitude for your faith—although it may seem weak at times—and for the faith of the community that sustains you in the midst of suffering.

+ In your spare time (!) memorize Miriam Kessler's poem.

"TRULY I TELL YOU, TODAY YOU WILL BE WITH ME IN PARADISE."

The Fourth Week of Lent:
THE FIFTH WORD

One of the criminals who were hanged there kept deriding him and saying, "Are you not the Messiah? Save yourself and us!" But the other rebuked him, saying, "Do you not fear God, since you are under the same sentence of condemnation? And we indeed have been condemned justly, for we are getting what we deserve for our deeds, but this man has done nothing wrong." Then he said, "Jesus, remember me when you come into your kingdom." He replied, *"Truly I tell you, today you will be with me in Paradise."* (Luke 23:39–43)

In the dreariness and death of a concentration camp, the psychiatrist Victor Frankl learned a simple but profound lesson that he shared in his book *Man's Search for Meaning*.[8] During his confinement in Theresienstadt, Auschwitz, Dachau, and finally Buchenwald, Frankl realized that he could not change his situation. What he could do, however, was to determine for himself in what spirit he was going to live with those circumstances.

In the gospel passage above, we have three men sentenced to death: a mix of innocence and guilt, and in their hearts, they, too, determine how to live with their suffering. On one cross, a man clings to anger and bitterness, lashing out and taunting the innocent man. On the second cross, the Good Thief, as he is often called, speaks in honesty and humility: "[W]e are getting what we deserve for our deeds, but this man has done nothing wrong....Jesus, remember me when you come into your kingdom" (Luke 23:41, 42). And the third man, Jesus, the innocent sufferer, hears the request of the man who asks to be remembered. Jesus responds, "Truly I tell you, today you will be with me in Paradise."

We do not choose many of the circumstances of our lives. The givens are so often given without consultation. The pain, the loss, and the uncertainties of our lives don't ask for permission to enter, but we may choose how to live with them. In the dying Jesus, we see compassion and mercy poured out. They are human characteristics when we are at our best. Let us pray to live them, even when we may be at our suffering worst.

What *hope* this scene holds for us! Despite his criminal story, the Good Thief must have kept alive in his heart a basic instinct for justice and compassion. That instinct becomes real when, in his suffering, he reaches out in kindness and in a kind of prayer to Jesus. No one of us can foresee how we'll die. I suspect that most of us hope for a peaceful scene in which we are surrounded by our loved ones and have received the sacraments that the church offers us, with all the loose ends of our lives finally tied up. Still, our prayer will be much the same as the Good Thief prayed: "Jesus, remember me." And we pray to experience what Jesus offers the Good Thief: "Today you will be with me in Paradise."

Each day this week:

+ Try to set aside fifteen minutes. Have you found a time that is most conducive to prayer? Maybe you'll have to rise earlier or stay up later than the others in your house in order to have quiet time and space.

+ Notice your breathing. As you inhale, ask for the Spirit to fill you.

+ Read the selection from Luke 23:39–43. Try to imagine that scene, putting yourself at the foot of the cross.

+ You may want to speak openly with Jesus or with the Good Thief.

+ At the conclusion of your prayer time, express your gratitude for the time that you've had with God.

+ Do you have a practice now of remembering the word for the week? Do you find that you're able to call it to mind when your mind is idle? Or does it come to you unbidden?

"[D]istractions in prayer are as normal and ordinary as they are in any relationship. You can be with someone you deeply love and be in a deep conversation and suddenly wonder if you put out the lights in the car. So, too, in prayer. Also distractions with a friend sometimes come because you do not want to hear what the friend is saying or because you are bored with the friend. The same thing can happen during prayer. Finally, if prayer is just conscious relationship, it is not something esoteric for saints and mystics. It is open to anyone, including the likes of us." (William A. Barry, SJ: *God and You: Prayer as a Personal Relationship*) [9]

Here are some thoughts and questions for your consideration—if they're helpful.

+ Recall how your own attitude toward suffering or toward a difficult situation has either helped or hindered you.

+ Remember those who are dying. Pray especially for those who feel alienated from God: that they will be free to respond lovingly.

+ In the Hail Mary, we ask her to intercede for us "now and at the hour of our death." Does that particular line hold much meaning for you?

The Fourth Week of Lent

✦ Reflect on the love that Jesus has for us, the love that invites us to be with him.

✦ At the outset of Lent, you had a particular desire as you began this book; has that desire sharpened or changed during the ensuing weeks?

"FATHER, INTO YOUR HANDS I COMMEND MY SPIRIT."

The Fifth Week of Lent:
THE SIXTH WORD

Then Jesus, crying with a loud voice, said, *"Father, into your hands I commend my spirit."* Having said this, he breathed his last. (Luke 23:46)

The four evangelists put different words on the lips of Jesus on the cross. In Luke's Gospel, the above are the last words that Jesus utters before he dies. They capture the final handing over. Jesus can do no more. He has given all to the care of his Father.

I think that most of us know similar moments—not perhaps of facing our own imminent death (although perhaps some of us have done that)—but moments of facing situations over which we have no control, even though we are highly invested in them. It may be the illness or death of loved ones, and we stand face to face with that which may steal them from us and we just don't know how life will go on. It may be the question of where we will work or study or live, and we come to see how limited is our control over the consequences of our decision. It may be at any moment when we have done all that was asked of us, and yet we know that the results are out of our hands. In those moments, we, like Jesus, face the starkness of our limitations.

In this moment, Jesus turns to the Father and prays. His prayer is from Psalm 31. It is a psalm of one who is seeking refuge. God is described as a rock and a fortress, the locus of security and protection. And the supplicant in it prays: "Into your hand I commit my spirit" (Ps 31:5). He prays: "My times are in your hand; deliver me from the hand of my enemies and persecutors" (Ps 31:15).

It is not necessarily easy to arrive at the point of handing all things over to God. We are taught again and again to be responsible for what we do. In our American culture, independence is prized. We speak about "the self made man/woman" as if anyone could really *make* himself or herself and then carry on without the aid of a massive network of people who help to "make the world go round."

The recognition of our lack of control may come slowly; but in accepting it and in handing all things over to God, there is a great freedom and a restoration to the true order. God is God and we are not. A simple truth, but sometimes we fight it mightily.

Each day this week:

+ Try to set aside fifteen minutes.

+ "Once, when asked how to pray, a wise spiritual teacher said, 'Pick a time, pick a place, and then show up" (Timothy Jones in *Workday Prayers*).[10] This is not to be confused with Woody Allen's "80 percent of success is showing up," although the point is the same!

+ Ask for the Holy Spirit to help you to pray.

+ Reread the above gospel selection. Be attentive to the scene, imagining it, putting yourself at the foot of the cross. You may want to speak with Jesus.

+ At the conclusion of your prayer, express your gratitude for the time that you've had, for "showing up."

+ This week, as you make your rounds of the usual things in your life, call this word to mind. Pray it when you realize that events in your own life are out of your control.

+ Be grateful for the Spirit's gift: that you desire to pray.

Some other thoughts that you might find to be helpful:

+ Try to enter this prayer with Jesus. Recall the deep relationship he had with his Father.

✦ Practice "let[ting] the same mind be in you that was in Christ Jesus" (Phil 2:5), in which you hand over to the Father the many worries that you carry. Sometimes they may be significant; oftentimes they aren't, but they drain our energy. Practice handing them over.

✦ Pray the words of Jesus on behalf of and with the dying: that they will be free to go to God.

✦ Consider world events. We see such tragic news on a regular basis, but we usually feel unable to do much about it. Focus on *one* picture or *one* story that touches your heart and pray for those people, entrusting them to God's care. You might be moved to action.

✦ Whenever you feel that life is beating you, you might find consolation in Psalm 31.

"IT IS FINISHED."

The Sixth Week of Lent (Holy Week):
THE SEVENTH WORD

When Jesus had received the wine, he said,
"It is finished." Then he bowed his head
and gave up his spirit. (John 19:30)

Of all the seven last words, the words, "It is finished,"
sound more like words of self-reflection than any others.
They are not like the interactive words spoken to Mary and
John; neither are they like the reconciling words spoken to
the repentant thief; nor, it seems, are they like the words of
anguish and committal addressed to the Father. Instead,
these words seem to be those of a man who, at the point of
dying, looks back at his living to see it as a unified whole. He
has come to do the will of the One who sent him. That is
what has sustained him. Jesus names the doing of his Father's
will as his food (John 4:34). In his last utterance, "It is finished," he sees not the end of his suffering, but rather the
completion of that for which he came: to do the Father's will.

Perhaps you, too, have tried to be faithful to God's will, and it is a struggle. The example of Jesus reminds us that the effort to be faithful may exact a price, and it may be unknown to most of those around you. The price may be in friendships broken; in money lost; or criticisms received. If you can look to your life as an effort to do God's will, then you may be able to draw strength from this example of fidelity that Jesus gives.

John's Gospel, unlike Matthew's and Mark's Gospels, recounts no dramatic events at this moment of death. There is no earthquake; no rending of the Temple curtain; yet it is a defining moment of salvation and inspiration. Jesus gives up his spirit, setting the stage for the sending of the Holy Spirit. Something new *is* possible because of his death. We have seen how that happens in the lives of other great people. Henri Nouwen once said: "The more we live, the more our deaths reveal the spirit that was there and that spirit can then continue to inform. Very simply that is what saints are all about. That is why Thomas Merton and Dorothy Day and all these people are sometimes more effective after their death than they were in life."[11]

Oscar Romero, the archbishop of El Salvador, also comes to mind. I suspect very few people outside of El Salvador knew anything about him until he was assassinated while saying Mass. He had become the voice of the poor; he had taken on their suffering and shared in their indignities. He understood that if he died for the cause, he would rise again in the Salvadoran people and his spirit of holiness would live on.

Holy Week is a rich opportunity for prayer. If you are able to attend the liturgies of the Triduum, the three days of Thursday, Friday, and Saturday, you may find yourself being attentive to the words and symbols and actions, particularly to the veneration of the cross on Good Friday, in a new way.

During Holy Week, we hear the reading of the passion twice: on Sunday and on Friday. The Sunday reading will come from the evangelist of the Cycle for year A or B or C. The Good Friday reading is always from the Gospel of John. You will hear some of the seven last words, though not all of them.

Each day this week:

+ If possible, try to set aside your usual fifteen minutes for prayer, even though you may also be spending time praying liturgically at the services of the Triduum. Ask for the Spirit's help. There may be a hymn that's particularly pertinent to Holy Week or a breathing exercise that helps you to move into stillness.

+ Recall the gospel scene and the words of Jesus: John 19:30. Try to be attentive to that scene.

Seven Last Words for Seven Weeks

✦ At the conclusion of your prayer time, express your gratitude for the time that you've had. You may want to write down your reflections for this word.

✦ Call this word to mind while you're preparing for church, when you're shopping or walking. Join yourself to Jesus as you're completing a task, saying in your own simple way, "It is finished," and giving thanks for what you have accomplished.

✦ You may also find that some parts of the liturgies are touching you, or you may be drawn back to a word that you reflected on previously. Keep that memory of how you have been touched, and return to it in quiet prayer.

✦ The most important advice continues to be the same: Don't get discouraged. Do the best you can.

Here again are some thoughts and questions for your consideration. As always, use them if they're helpful, but disregard them if they aren't.

✦ Can you look back on your life and see a pattern? Can you see how God's will has been at work in it?

✦ Are there some specific aspects to your life that you can look back on and say, "It is finished," and pray in thanksgiving?

The Sixth Week of Lent

✦ How does the example of the fidelity of Jesus touch you?

✦ Spend some time reflecting on how this Lenten season and this practice of keeping one word for a week has helped you to pray and to prepare for the season of Easter.

CONCLUSION

During the Easter season, as you continue to celebrate the resurrection, remember your desire for prayer. Continue to ask for God's help to pray. Recall what you've learned about how and where and when you've prayed. As the season stretches out over the next weeks (the Easter season, too, is seven weeks long), perhaps you will hear or read a word or phrase in the Sunday scripture passages that you will carry with you each of those seven weeks.

Beyond the Easter season, into Ordinary Time, and throughout each of the liturgical seasons, may you continue to find nourishment in Christ's words, for as the Easter Vigil reminds us,

> *Christ yesterday and today*
> *the beginning and the end*
> *Alpha*
> *and Omega*
> *all time belongs to him*
> *and all the ages*
> *to him be glory and power*
> *through every age for ever. Amen.*[12]

Notes

1. I described this experience in an article in the February 14, 2002, edition of *Church World*, the newspaper for the Diocese of Portland, Maine.

2. Lawrence Martin Jenco, OSM, *Bound to Forgive: The Pilgrimage to Reconciliation of a Beirut Hostage* (Notre Dame: Ave Maria Press, 1995), 14.

3. James F. Clarity, "20,000 Rally in Dublin for Peace in North and Against I.R.A. Killing," *New York Times*, March 29, 1993.

4. Father Connell's Confraternity Edition *New Baltimore Catechism* No. 3 (New York: Benziger Brothers, 1949), 281.

5. Edward Farrell, *Prayer Is a Hunger* (Denville, NJ: Dimensions, 1972).

6. Miriam Kessler, "Eli, Eli," in *Cries of the Spirit*, Marilyn Sewell, ed (Boston: Beacon Press, 1991), 256.

7. James Carroll, *Prayer from Where We Are* (Dayton: Pflaum Publishing, 1970), 32.

8. Viktor Frankl, *Man's Search for Meaning* (New York: Simon and Schuster, 1962).

Notes

9. William A. Barry, SJ, *God and You: Prayer as a Personal Relationship* (Mahwah, NJ: Paulist Press, 1987), 15.

10. Timothy Jones, *Workday Prayers* (Chicago: Loyola Press, 2000), 257.

11. Henri Nouwen, in an interview with *National Catholic Reporter*, April 1, 1994 (v30, n22): 11.

12. *The Sacramentary* (New York: Catholic Book Publishing, 1985), 172.

Bibliography

Barry, William A., SJ. *God and You: Prayer as a Personal Relationship.* Mahwah, NJ: Paulist Press, 1987.

———*Seek My Face: Prayer as a Personal Relationship in Scripture.* Mahwah, NJ: Paulist Press, 1989.

———*What Do I Want in Prayer?* Mahwah, NJ: Paulist Press, 1994.

Culbertson, Diana, ed. *Invisible Light: Poems about God.* New York: Columbia University Press, 2000.

Farrell, Edward. *Prayer Is a Hunger.* Denville, NJ: Dimensions, 1972.

Gardner, W.H., ed. *Poems and Prose of Gerard Manley Hopkins.* Baltimore: Penguin Books, 1963.

Green, Thomas H., SJ. *Opening to God.* Notre Dame: Ave Maria Press, 1977.

Healey, Charles J., SJ. *A New Song to the Lord.* New York: Alba House, 1991.

———*Christian Spirituality.* New York: Alba House, 1999.

Jenco, Lawrence Martin, OSM. *Bound to Forgive: The Pilgrimage to Reconciliation of a Beirut Hostage.* Notre Dame: Ave Maria Press, 1995.

Jones, Timothy. *Workday Prayers: On-the-Job-Meditations for Tending Your Soul.* Chicago: Loyola Press, 2000.

Bibliography

Ladinsky, Daniel, ed. *Love Poems from God: Twelve Sacred Voices from the East and West.* New York: Penguin Compass, 2002.

Nouwen, Henri J.M. *Spiritual Journals.* New York: Continuum Publishing Co., 1997.

————*With Open Hands.* Notre Dame: Ave Maria Press, 1972.

Sewell, Marilyn, ed. *Cries of the Spirit.* Boston: Beacon Press, 1991.

Sheldrake, Philip, SJ. *Befriending Our Desires.* Notre Dame: Ave Maria Press, 1994.

Van Breeman, Peter G. *As Bread that Is Broken.* Denville, NJ: Dimension Books, 1974.

Zagano, Phyllis. *On Prayer.* Mahwah, NJ: Paulist Press, 1994.